Jackie Robinson

by Jill C. Wheeler

visit us at
www.abdopub.com

Published by ABDO & Daughters, an imprint of ABDO Publishing Company, 4940 Viking Drive, Suite 622, Edina, Minnesota 55435. Copyright ©2003 by Abdo Consulting Group, Inc. International copyrights reserved in all countries. No part of this book may be reproduced in any form without written permission from the publisher.

Printed in the United States.

Edited by Paul Joseph
Graphic Design: John Hamilton
Cover Design: Mighty Media
Interior Photos: AP/Photo, p. 1, 9, 11, 28, 31, 34, 38, 43, 49, 55, 57, 58, 61
Corbis, p. 5, 7, 12, 15, 17, 19, 21, 22, 25, 27, 33, 37, 40, 45, 46, 51, 53

Library of Congress Cataloging-in-Publication Data

Wheeler, Jill C., 1964-
Jackie Robinson / Jill C. Wheeler.
p. cm. — (Breaking barriers)
Includes index.
Summary: A biography of the first African American to break the color barrier in major league baseball.
ISBN 1-57765-739-X
1. Robinson, Jackie, 1919-1972—Juvenile literature. 2. Baseball players—United States—Biography—Juvenile literature. 3. African American baseball players—Biography—Juvenile literature. [1. Robinson, Jackie, 1919-1972. 2. Baseball players. 3. African Americans—Biography.] I. Title.

GV865.R6 W48 2002
796.357'092—dc21
[B]

2001046116

Contents

Jackie's Inspiration

*I*n the summer of 1936, people around the world focused on Berlin, Germany. The International Olympic Committee had chosen Berlin for the site of the summer Olympics. The world's greatest athletes traveled to Germany to compete.

During this time, Adolf Hitler ruled Germany. He believed white people, and thus white athletes, were superior to all others. Because of this, some people wanted to boycott the Olympics. But others thought it would be better to prove that Hitler and other racist people were wrong. They wanted to show that no race or ethnicity was superior to another.

Two of the U.S. contenders in the men's 200-meter dash were African-Americans. Jesse Owens won the gold medal, and Mack Robinson won the silver medal. Like Owens, Mack Robinson was the grandson of slaves. And like Owens, he was the son of sharecroppers. Robinson returned to the United States an Olympic hero. But because he was black, no one would give him a good job. The man who won a silver medal for the United States had to take a job as a street sweeper.

Jesse Owens wins the 200-meter dash at the final Olympic tryouts at Randall's Island, New York, July 12, 1936. Mack Robinson, far left, placed second.

Mack's younger brother, Jackie, felt Mack deserved better. He felt all African-Americans deserved a chance to compete equally against whites. It didn't matter whether it was in sports or the workplace. Jackie was proud of his brother for competing in the Olympics. Jackie thought that it was unfair that people treated Mack poorly when he returned to the United States. Jackie wanted to improve the treatment of African-Americans.

And that's exactly what he would end up doing. He would become the first African-American to break the color barrier in major league baseball. In doing so, he would help open the world of professional athletics for all African-Americans.

Sharecroppers' Son

Jack Roosevelt Robinson was born on January 31, 1919, on a farm near Cairo, Georgia. He was the grandson of slaves, but his parents, Jerry and Mallie Robinson, were free. They did not own any land. Instead, they worked someone else's land as sharecroppers. This meant that in exchange for doing the farmwork, they received a share of the profits.

Jackie was the baby of the family. He had three older brothers, Edgar, Frank, and Mack. He also had an older sister, Willa Mae. When Jackie was only six months old, his father decided that he couldn't handle life on the farm anymore. He told Mallie that he was going to visit his brother in Texas. The family never saw him again.

Mallie could not run the farm without help, so the owner became angry with her. In the spring of 1921, she loaded the family on to a train and set out for California. Mallie's brother lived there. Mallie hoped her young family could get a fresh start in Southern California.

Jackie Robinson

The Robinsons moved into a three-room apartment in Pasadena, California. They shared the small quarters with Mallie's brother, and Mallie's sister's family. Mallie found a job as a maid for a white family. She would get up before dawn and return to the house exhausted. Despite this, she still found time to spend with her children. Mallie made sure all of her children learned the importance of being a family, getting a good education, going to church, and caring for others.

Mallie saved enough money to buy her family a house on Pepper Street in Pasadena. The two-story house had five bedrooms. So the family had a lot more space and privacy. The Robinson children called it the Castle.

Life at the Castle was far from royal. The Robinsons were the only African-Americans on the street. California was less segregated than Georgia, but African-Americans still received unequal treatment. Many of the white people on Pepper Street wanted the Robinsons to leave. They taunted the Robinson children and called them names. Some neighbors even tried to buy the house from the family.

Mallie had her hands full in those days. Her job left her little time to watch Jackie. Willa Mae became a second mom to him. When Willa Mae went to school, no one was able to watch Jackie. He was too young to stay home by himself. So Willa Mae brought him with her to Grover Cleveland Elementary School.

Willa Mae told him to play in the sandbox while she was in class. The teacher allowed Willa Mae to sit next to a window so she could watch her little brother. When it rained, the teacher allowed Jackie to come inside and sit in the kindergarten classroom.

Jackie Robinson was honored on a commemorative stamp in 1999. The stamp was part of the U.S. Postal Service's "Celebrate the Century" program.

King of the Playground

The Robinsons had little money. Mallie couldn't afford to buy her children many toys. So they learned to entertain themselves. Often, that meant playing sports.

Jackie's sister and brothers were all natural athletes. He often played with them and their friends. At school, Jackie soon became one of the most popular players. He was incredibly fast. It wasn't long before children at school bribed Jackie to be on their team. They offered him food from their lunches if he would play on their side.

By now, the United States was enduring the Great Depression. It was harder than ever for Mallie to pay all the family's bills. Jackie and his siblings worked to earn extra money for the family. Jackie worked at a variety of odd jobs. He sold hot dogs at a nearby stadium, cut grass, and ran errands. He also had a newspaper route.

Jackie Robinson was an infielder for the Brooklyn Dodgers when this photo was taken in 1952.

When he was in high school, Jackie and his friends would sometimes spend their hard-earned money at the movies. There, Jackie got to see one of his heroes, African-American boxer Joe Louis. At the movies, Jackie and his friends had to sit in the back of the theater. Only whites were allowed to sit in the front. Yet Jackie watched Joe Louis compete equally against his white opponent on the screen.

A movie theater in the 1930s with a rear entrance for people of color.

Jackie wasn't the only one feeling the sting of racism. In his teen years, he began hanging out with other young men of color in the neighborhood. They formed the Pepper Street gang. The Pepper Street gang members were African-American, Asian, and Hispanic. They felt that white people had advantages over them, so they banded together. Jackie became their leader.

Sometimes the Pepper Street gang got into trouble, but it was rarely serious. Jackie's gang stole golf balls off of the golf course, and then sold them back to the golfers. Sometimes the gang threw rocks or dirt clods at cars. Once they put sticky, black tar on someone's lawn. Mallie learned about the prank and forced Jackie to clean it up.

Jackie might have stayed with the Pepper Street gang and gotten into even more trouble. However, two men helped him turn his life around. A local mechanic named Carl Anderson befriended Jackie. He showed Jackie how staying in the gang would hurt him and his family. In addition, Pastor Karl Downs at the Robinson family's church stepped in to help. Like Jackie, Pastor Downs loved sports. Downs started a church sports league. He encouraged Jackie to put his energy into athletics instead of into making mischief. It worked.

Aiming High

While Jackie made a name for himself at school, his brother Mack became a national track star. Mack's silver medal in the men's 200-meter dash at the 1936 Olympics inspired Jackie. Jackie decided to make athletics his ticket out of poverty. He played tennis, golf, softball, football, and basketball. He also competed in track. Jackie excelled at whatever sport he played.

As Jackie grew older, he became an even better athlete. He earned a reputation as a fierce competitor at John Muir Technical High School. There, he won letters in football, basketball, track, and baseball. In football, Jackie played running back and quarterback. In basketball, he led the team in rebounding and scoring. On the baseball diamond, he slammed out powerful hits and stole bases in the wink of an eye.

After graduating from high school, Jackie enrolled at Pasadena Junior College. Mack also had attended that college. Jackie had a great deal of respect for Mack, and wanted to follow in his footsteps. At Pasadena Junior College, Jackie played football. In his freshman year, he broke his ankle in pre-season football practice. He had to sit out for the first four games. When Jackie returned, he took over as quarterback. The team won every remaining game.

UCLA quarterback Jackie Robinson, the college's first student-athlete to earn varsity letters in four different sports, leaps in the air to throw a pass.

In basketball, Jackie became Pasadena Junior College's top-scoring player. When basketball season ended, Jackie went out for both track and baseball. It was tough to juggle both sports. Sometimes baseball games and track meets happened at the same time. One day, Jackie competed in both a track meet and a championship baseball game. He had a flat tire on the way to the track meet. Arriving late, he didn't have the chance to warm up before competing in the broad jump. He recorded an astonishing jump of 25 feet and six and one-half inches that day. He had set a new school record. Jackie's brother Mack had set the old record.

Jackie immediately left the track meet and hurried to another city to join the baseball game that had already started. It was the California Junior College Baseball Championship. Jackie played shortstop, and at bat he slammed out two hits and stole a base to help lead his team to victory. Few people were surprised when Jackie was named the Most Valuable Junior College Player in Southern California in 1938. Some people said Jackie was the best athlete in all of Southern California.

Pasadena Junior College only had a two-year program. As Jackie's time there wound down, scouts from other universities paid close attention to him.

Many scouts wanted him to play for their teams. They made Jackie tempting offers.

Jackie turned to his brother Frank for guidance. Frank always had been Jackie's biggest fan. Jackie did not want to go to college far away from home. So with Frank's help, Jackie chose the University of California at Los Angeles (UCLA).

Frank never got to see Jackie's accomplishments at UCLA. He died following a motorcycle accident in the spring of 1939. Jackie began classes at UCLA that fall. Over the next two years, he became the university's first four-letter athlete. He earned letters in football, basketball, baseball, and track. With every accomplishment, Jackie kept Frank in his thoughts. He still wanted to make his brother proud.

Jackie Robinson runs upfield during a UCLA football game.

College Days

While Jackie could play virtually every sport, his favorite was football. As the UCLA team entered the 1939 season, they were not expected to do well. However, they had a new special weapon. That was Jackie. In the third game of the season, against Stanford University, Jackie ran 52 yards for a touchdown. After the game, the Stanford coach said Jackie was the greatest backfield runner he'd seen in 25 years of coaching. The UCLA Bruins narrowly lost a spot in the Rose Bowl that year.

Further praise followed in Jackie's second year at UCLA. The star of the basketball team, Jackie led the Pacific Coast Conference, Southern Division, in scoring. However, he did not make the all-conference team. Some believed it was because he was an African-American.

Jackie didn't do as well in baseball. The exception was the first game of the season, when he stole four bases and had four hits. The rest of the games went poorly for Jackie. He ended the season with a batting average of .097.

Midair action of UCLA student Jackie Robinson winning the long jump at a track meet at the Los Angeles Coliseum in 1940.

Life at UCLA wasn't always easy for Jackie. Jackie never had been one to take racism sitting down. As an African-American, he frequently had to stand up to taunting and name-calling. He was proud of his abilities, and he was proud of the color of his skin. On the playing field, he was a fierce competitor. As a result, some people thought he was a troublemaker.

In reality, Jackie was very shy. Even though he was handsome and athletic, he'd never really had a girlfriend. Many girls wanted to meet him because he was a star athlete. Jackie didn't want a girlfriend who was only interested in that part of his life.

Things changed in his second year at UCLA. A friend introduced Jackie to a young nursing student named Rachel Isum. Rachel had heard about Jackie. She assumed he was arrogant, but as she got to know him she realized he wasn't. Rachel became his steady girlfriend. Jackie enjoyed dating someone who appreciated him.

Jackie surprised Rachel a few months later by announcing that he was leaving UCLA. He had decided to get a job and earn money. He felt that his mother had been supporting the family long enough. He wanted to help. His coaches tried to convince him to stay, but he had made up his mind. He applied to work at a youth camp and got the job.

Jackie Robinson was a fierce competitor on the UCLA football team.

The battleships USS West Virginia *and* Tennessee *burn after the Japanese surprise attack on Pearl Harbor.*

Jackie enjoyed his work at the youth camp. It didn't pay much, though. When the program got canceled, he decided to try playing football. He wanted to play professional football so he could earn a better salary. At that time, though, blacks were not welcome in professional football. Instead, Jackie joined a semi-professional football team in Hawaii.

Jackie returned to California in early December 1941. Two days after he left Honolulu, Japanese bombers attacked the U.S. Pacific Fleet at Pearl Harbor. The United States was pulled into World War II. And so was Jackie.

Lieutenant Robinson

Like millions of other young American men, Robinson entered the U.S. Army to serve his country. In April 1942, the army sent him to Fort Riley, Kansas, for basic training. Robinson decided he wanted to be an officer. He applied for Officers' Candidate School. Robinson did not hear back from the school for a long time.

After a while, Robinson learned the army didn't like having black officers. This was racism, and Robinson wanted to fight it. He knew he would need help if he were to succeed. Help came in the form of heavyweight boxing champion Joe Louis. Louis was transferred to Fort Riley while Robinson was there, and the two became friends. Louis used his connections to help Robinson get into Officers' Candidate School.

Lieutenant Jackie Robinson in his U.S. Army uniform.

In January 1943, Robinson became a second lieutenant. To celebrate, he bought an engagement ring for Rachel, or Rae, as he called her. He had been writing to Rae almost every day since he left UCLA. Rae also had gone to work for the war effort. She had moved to San Francisco, where she worked nights in an aircraft factory. During the day, Rae continued to study nursing.

Despite becoming an officer, Robinson still faced racism. At that time, the U.S. Army was segregated. Black and white soldiers had separate barracks and separate sections in cafeterias. Robinson wanted to play on the army baseball team at Fort Riley, but he was not allowed. The army did want him on the football team, however. He refused. Robinson believed that if he was good enough for football, then he should be good enough for baseball. That is just one of the many ways that Robinson stood up for himself and for all African-Americans.

Army officials did not appreciate Robinson's views. They also didn't appreciate how he was trying to improve things for the African-American soldiers under his command. The army transferred him to Camp Hood, Texas.

Soldiers of the 4505-C, 780th MP Battalion. The battalion, which was comprised mostly of African-American troops, contained 90 college graduates and 15 Ph.D.s.

A segregated bus in Atlanta, Georgia, in 1956.

It wasn't long before Robinson ran into trouble in Texas. He was riding in a bus at Camp Hood when the bus driver demanded he move to one of the seats at the back of the bus. In those days, most places in the South had rules that said blacks had to ride in the back of buses. Yet Robinson knew the army had finally issued a rule stating blacks could ride wherever they wanted while on army bases. He knew his rights, so he stayed where he was.

Robinson was arrested and court-martialed. He was cleared of all charges in August 1944. In November, he requested a medical discharge because of the bone chips he had in his ankle from his college football injury. Robinson received an honorable discharge. He was relieved. He'd had enough of the army.

Barnstorming Days

Robinson now was 25 years old. He needed to find a job that paid enough for him to marry Rachel and settle down. He still wanted to play professional football. Yet he knew it was not an option due to the color barrier in professional sports. His best option was to become a coach. In January 1945, he took a job coaching basketball at a small black college in Texas. He quickly realized that the job was not for him. He needed something different.

Robinson remembered a conversation he'd had while still in the army. He had met a player with the Kansas City Monarchs baseball team. The Monarchs were part of the Negro American League. The player had seen Robinson field a baseball. He had told Robinson that the team was looking for good players. Robinson contacted the team. In April 1945, he got a job playing baseball for $400 a month.

Jackie Robinson with the Kansas City Monarchs in 1945.

The Negro American League and the Negro National League were the only professional baseball leagues for black players. Being a member of a league meant a hard life on the road. The teams didn't own any stadiums. They had to play at the white teams' stadiums, or find other areas. They would ride buses from town to town, playing wherever and whenever they could find a place. As a result, they often had to play at strange times, or play up to four games in a single day. Players called these on-the-fly games barnstorming. In 1929, the black leagues were the first to play baseball at night using electric lights that they brought with them. The first night game in the majors wasn't until 1935.

The black leagues' games drew white and black fans alike. At that time, few people had televisions. The only way to see a game live was to go to it. It was great for fans, as many people had the chance to see live baseball. Yet it was very hard on the players. They would spend weeks at a time on the road, sleeping on the bus, on bleachers, or even on the ground. Even worse, many restaurants in those days would not serve blacks. That meant the barnstormers even had to eat on the bus.

A Newark Eagles player rounds first base during a game against the New York Black Yankees.

Kansas City Monarchs pitching great Satchel Paige warms up at New York's Yankee Stadium in 1942 for a game between the Monarchs and the New York Cuban Stars.

Despite the hardships, the all-black leagues produced some of the finest players in the history of the game. Players such as Satchel Paige, Josh Gibson, and Cool Papa Bell lit up the black league games. Today, many fans believe such players would have dominated the major leagues, had they been allowed to play.

Rae was not happy when Robinson told her he was going barnstorming. She wanted to settle down to a normal life. But Robinson assured her it was only temporary. He said he would make good money, and then he would quit baseball.

Robinson had an excellent opportunity to perfect his skills while playing with the Monarchs. He finessed his base-stealing skills by watching Cool Papa Bell. Robinson received several helpful tips from other ballplayers as well. Baseball had never been his strongest sport, so he needed practice.

During his first season with the Monarchs, Robinson proved to be a great hitter, slamming out ten doubles, four triples, and five home runs. Fans quickly took note of the new rookie. So did the major league scouts.

Branch Rickey

Virtually everyone in major league baseball had to admit that the all-black leagues had a great deal of talent. Yet only a handful of those people had the desire to see those talents come into the all-white major leagues. One of those people was a man named Branch Rickey.

Rickey worked as the president and general manager of the Brooklyn Dodgers. He had been in baseball for nearly 40 years, as a player, coach, and manager. As a manager, he had created a string of winning teams. He wanted to do the same for the Dodgers, and that meant finding new talent. He used a large team of scouts to watch games around the country and identify promising players.

Rickey believed there was tremendous talent in the black leagues. The challenge was finding a way to integrate major league baseball. For Rickey, it was more than a professional duty. It was a personal quest. Rickey never forgot the time he was a college baseball coach with one black player on his team. The team had traveled to an away game, and the hotel they visited refused to let the black player stay. Rickey finally got the hotel to let the player stay in Rickey's room. He never forgot how the injustice had made that player feel. He vowed to do all he could to stop that kind of treatment for African-American athletes.

Branch Rickey was a player and coach for many years before moving up to manager.

Branch Rickey

Rickey knew he had to make his plans carefully. In 1943, he began talking about signing up a black player. He told skeptics he *might* have to do it for the good of the team. In reality, he was determined to do it. He took another step in 1945. He told reporters he was thinking about starting yet another all-black league. That gave him an excuse to send his scouts to the black leagues' games.

One name kept popping up again and again on the scouting reports. It was Jackie Robinson. In August 1945, Rickey arranged a meeting with the 26-year-old player. Robinson thought he was going to talk with Rickey about his new all-black league. Rickey quickly told him that wasn't the case. He wanted to know if Robinson could handle being the first African-American to play in the major leagues.

For the next three hours, Rickey grilled Robinson about his personal life, his opinions, and how he thought he would react in a variety of situations. Rickey wasn't too concerned about Robinson's talents on the baseball diamond. He knew Robinson was a great player. What he wanted to know was could Robinson take the abuse that would go with becoming the first black in the major leagues? Could he keep his cool when fans called him names? When pitchers intentionally threw balls at him? When base runners deliberately gouged him with their spikes?

Jackie Robinson signs a contract with Brooklyn Dodgers team president Branch Rickey.

Robinson listened intently. Finally he asked, "Rickey, are you looking for a Negro who is afraid to fight back?" Rickey replied, "I am looking for a ballplayer with guts enough not to fight back."

Robinson considered Rickey's offer. He had begun to like Rickey, and he appreciated what he was trying to do. Robinson realized he had to do it, not only for himself but also for all African-Americans. Finally, he gave Rickey an answer. "Mr. Rickey, I think I can play ball... If you want me to take this gamble, I promise you there will be no incident."

On October 23, 1945, the Dodgers announced they had signed Robinson to their farm team, the Montreal Royals. Rickey had taken the first swing at the major league color barrier.

Montreal

In February 1946, Robinson and Rae got married in Los Angeles, California. Robinson's old friend Pastor Karl Downs performed the ceremony. Soon the Robinsons headed to Daytona Beach, Florida, for the Montreal farm club's spring training camp.

Their troubles began as soon as they hit the road. They took a plane from Los Angeles to New Orleans, Louisiana. They had to get a hotel room because they were not allowed on their connecting flight at the original time. The South was still segregated. And the only hotel that would rent a room to a black couple was so dirty that neither of them wanted to stay there. To make matters worse, no restaurants would allow them to sit down at the tables.

The Robinsons finally caught their connecting flight to Daytona Beach. When it landed in Pensacola for refueling, airline officials asked them to give up their seats for white passengers. After that, the Robinsons decided to take a bus, where they were forced to sit in the less comfortable back section. The bus ride was 16 hours long. The Robinsons arrived in Daytona Beach tired, hungry, and late for spring training.

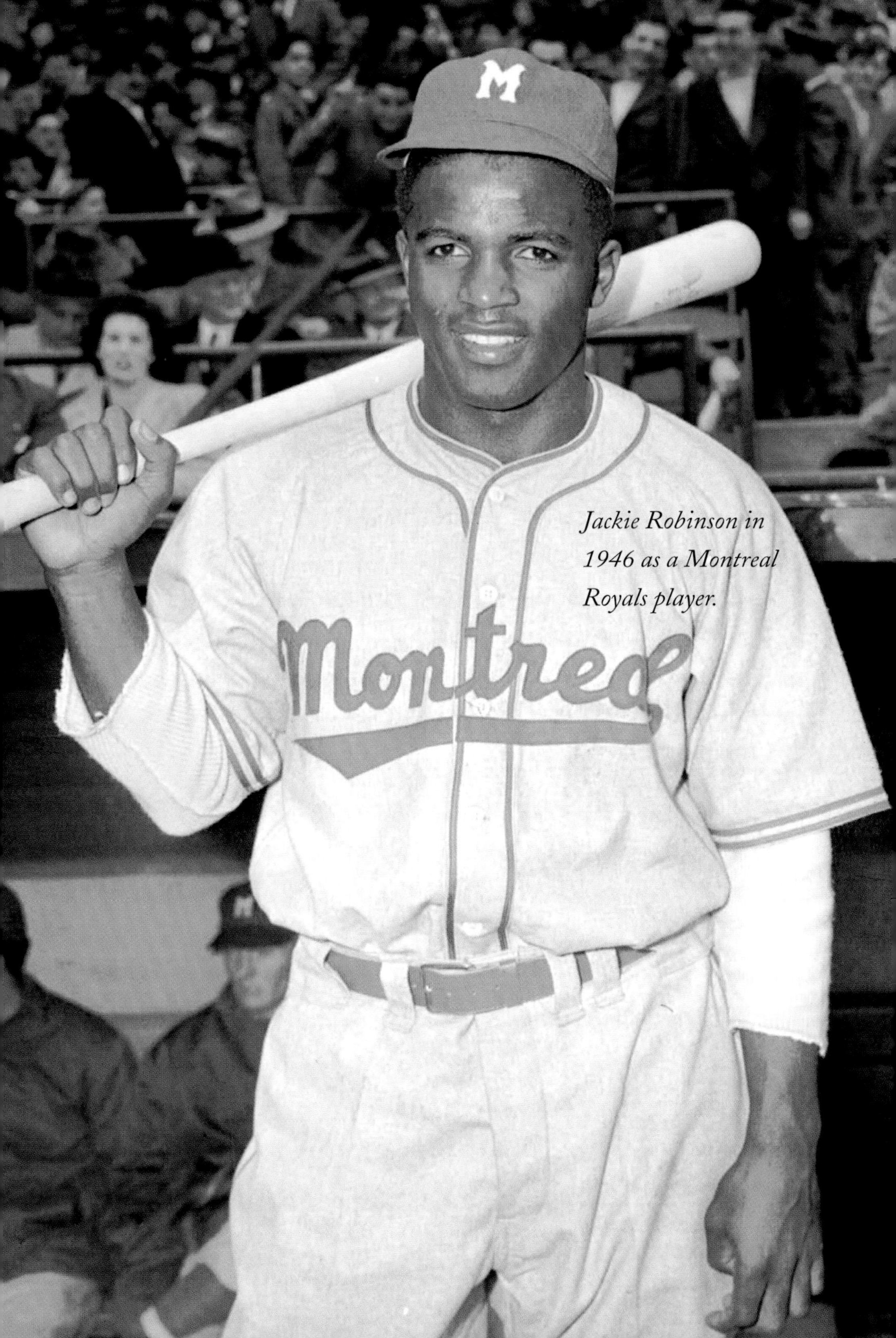

Jackie Robinson in 1946 as a Montreal Royals player.

Already, some people were against Robinson. The first game, scheduled for Jacksonville, Florida, was canceled. City officials said they had a law that stated blacks and whites couldn't play together on city-owned ball fields. Another time, a city police officer walked onto the playing field and said Robinson had to be removed to keep the peace. Remembering his promise to Rickey, Robinson quietly went with the officer.

Meanwhile, Robinson had plenty of other things on his mind. He had to try out to make the Montreal team. He was nervous and tried too hard, ending up with a sore arm. He ended the exhibition season with little to cheer about. Many people doubted that he would be up to the challenge of playing in the majors.

The test came on April 18, 1946. It was Robinson's first regular season game. The Royals were playing the Jersey City Giants in Jersey City, New Jersey. Twenty-five thousand fans packed the stadium.

On his first trip to the plate, Robinson grounded out. Then in the top of the third inning, he slammed out a home run with two players on base. He scored two more times in the game on balks. Jackie Robinson was off to a winning start in the big leagues.

Montreal Royal Jackie Robinson stretches for a ball hit through the infield.

Jackie Robinson warms up before stepping to the plate as a Montreal Royal.

Thousands of people came to see Robinson play. Many hoped he would play well, because they knew it would help end racism. Robinson and his wife were able to find a nice apartment in Montreal, Canada. Unlike in the South, most people in Montreal treated the Robinsons courteously.

By the end of the season, Robinson was leading the league in batting, and the Royals were at the top of their division. Robinson also was worn out. He went to a doctor who told him he should stop playing baseball for a while. Robinson took exactly one day off before returning to the field. His dedication helped lead the Royals to a spot in the Little World Series. The Little World Series was the farm team version of the World Series.

The 1946 Little World Series paired the Royals with the Louisville Colonels of Louisville, Kentucky. This pairing meant Robinson had to play baseball in the South again. It was a difficult series for him. Fans booed Robinson during the first three games in Louisville. He played poorly. The Royals lost two of the three games. Robinson's luck changed when the team returned for the last games in Montreal. Robinson was among his fans again. Montreal won the last three games, and Robinson scored the winning run of the series. He was mobbed by fans who saw him not as a black person, but as a ballplayer.

Dodger at Last

On April 9, 1947, the Brooklyn Dodgers issued a press release. It said they had signed Jackie Robinson to play in the major leagues. Suddenly, Robinson had to prove himself all over again.

As before, trouble started immediately. Many of the other Dodger players signed a petition saying they refused to play with Robinson. Rickey quickly made it known that if they didn't want to play with Robinson, they could quit the team. Likewise, the Philadelphia Phillies said they wouldn't play, but in the end, they weren't willing to forfeit the game. The St. Louis Cardinals said they would not play the Dodgers because of Robinson, also. Their manager told them they would have to leave the league if they refused.

Players on opposing teams treated Robinson cruelly. More than one pitcher tried to hit Robinson when he was at bat. Base runners slid into Robinson at first base and tried to stab him with the spikes on their shoes. On the field and in the bleachers, both players and spectators hurled insults. At home, Robinson received threatening letters. Through it all, he kept his promise to Rickey and refused to fight back. Instead, he proved himself with his bat and glove.

Jackie Robinson in a Brooklyn Dodgers uniform .

In the beginning, Robinson played poorly. In the fifth game of the season, however, he finally came alive. He hit a single and stole three bases, including home, to win the game against the Phillies. The manager of the Phillies had told his players to pick on Robinson. Some of the Dodger players who had said they wouldn't play with Robinson began defending him. One was Eddie Stanky. He yelled to the Phillies "Why don't you yell at somebody who can answer back?" Robinson's ability and dedication to the team were getting results. His teammates were starting to respect him.

Robinson ended his first season with a .297 batting average and 12 home runs. He led the league in stolen bases, and his playing helped the Dodgers win the National League pennant. Perhaps best of all, Robinson was voted Rookie of the Year by some of the very people who said he could never survive as a major league player.

The end of November 1947 found Robinson relieved and excited. His son, Jackie, Jr., had been born that month. And, thanks to his groundbreaking efforts, the Dodgers signed another African-American, named Dan Bankhead, to their team. The Cleveland Indians also signed an African-American, Larry Doby, making the American League integrated at last. Negro Leagues' legend Satchel Paige received his chance to play in the majors in 1948 when he signed with the Indians. At age 42, he became baseball's oldest rookie.

Jackie Robinson slides in safe at home on a double steal.

Glory Days

The golden era for the Brooklyn Dodgers began in 1948, thanks to Robinson. That year he switched from playing first base to second base. He teamed up with shortstop Pee Wee Reese, and together they made double plays that won games and made fans go crazy. African-American fans loved seeing another African-American winning the respect and admiration of millions for his abilities.

By now, Rickey had told Robinson he could start fighting back. Robinson began to speak up for better treatment of blacks in the major leagues and everywhere else. He protested when he and the other blacks on the team were not allowed to stay in the same hotels as their teammates while on the road.

On the field, Robinson continued to rack up honors. He won the National League batting title and was named Most Valuable Player in 1949. With Robinson's help, the Dodgers won six National League pennants. By 1950, Robinson was earning $35,000 a year. That made him the highest-paid Dodger of any color. A movie was even made about his life, starring Robinson as himself.

Robinson and his wife had two more children after Jackie, Jr. In 1950, they had a baby girl named Sharon. And two years later, they had their last child, David. Now with three children, the Robinsons decided to move into a bigger home. Even though Robinson was famous, many white people did not want him in their neighborhood. Eventually they did find a nice home and started making new friends.

By 1955, Robinson's skills were starting to slow. He remained an important part of the team, however. He daringly stole home in the first game of the World Series against the New York Yankees. Even though they did not win that game, his move spurred the Dodgers on to win the World Series itself. It was their first World Series victory.

Jackie Robinson in action at second base.

A New Career

In 1957, the Dodgers announced they were moving to Los Angeles. Then they announced they were trading Robinson to the New York Giants. After 10 years, Robinson had too much loyalty to the Dodgers to play for anyone else. Also, he knew his career was nearly over.

Robinson decided to retire from baseball. He took a job as vice president of personnel with the Chock Full o' Nuts Corporation. Many African-Americans worked for the company. The white founder, Bill Black, supported blacks and their rights. When Robinson was asked to chair the Freedom Fund Drive for the National Association for the Advancement of Colored People (NAACP), Black supported him completely. He even gave him a large check for the cause.

Robinson became active in the NAACP. He traveled to raise money and awareness for the civil rights reform. Because he was a celebrity, many people listened. Finally he helped to start the Freedom National Bank in New York City. The bank made important loans to people of color that white-owned banks would not.

Jackie Robinson, retiring after a 10-year career, leaves the Dodgers' clubhouse after collecting his belongings for the last time on January 7, 1957.

Robinson also became involved in politics. He supported Republican Richard Nixon in his 1960 presidential bid against John Kennedy. Four years later, he worked for Republican Nelson Rockefeller. Many African-Americans criticized Robinson for supporting Republican candidates. They claimed Democratic candidates could do more to help African-Americans. But Robinson believed that African-Americans should be represented in both parties.

Though Robinson no longer played baseball, his fans did not forget him. In 1962, he became the first African-American elected to the baseball Hall of Fame. It was the highlight of an incredible athletic career. Branch Rickey was on hand to help celebrate the honor. Sadly, Rickey died three years later.

Soon many difficult events happened in Robinson's life. In 1968, Robinson's mother died. Then Jackie, Jr., returned from the war in Vietnam with an addiction to drugs. The Robinsons placed their son into a program to help him overcome the addiction. He triumphed and began to help other people with addictions. In 1971, he tragically died in a car accident.

Jackie Robinson became the first black player inducted into baseball's Hall of Fame on July 23, 1962.

Jackie Robinson in 1971.

By this time, Robinson's hair had turned white, and he looked much older than he was. He had diabetes and was fighting problems with his vision and his heart. He walked with a limp. Still, the major leagues remembered him. In June 1972, the Los Angeles Dodgers held a special day for him, when they retired his uniform, number 42.

That October, he enjoyed another honor. He was asked to throw out the first ball at the second game of the World Series. Nine days later, on October 24, 1972, Robinson died of a heart attack.

Robinson's spirit was honored once again on April 15, 1997. It was the fiftieth anniversary of his first major league game. President Bill Clinton joined Rae Robinson to retire jersey number 42 among all major league teams. It was a tribute to the man who had changed not only the game of baseball, but also the face of America.

Timeline

January 31, 1919: Jack Roosevelt Robinson is born in Cairo, Georgia.

1921: The Robinsons move to Pasadena, California.

1937-1939: Robinson attends Pasadena Junior College.

1939-1941: Robinson attends UCLA, becoming its first four-letter athlete.

1943: Robinson becomes a second lieutenant in the U.S. Army.

1945: Robinson plays with the Negro League's Kansas City Monarchs baseball team.

February 1946: Robinson marries Rachel Isum.

1946: Robinson plays with the Montreal Royals farm team.

1947: Robinson signs a contract with the Brooklyn Dodgers.

1957: Robinson retires from baseball and becomes involved with politics and the NAACP.

1962: Robinson becomes the first African-American to be inducted into the Baseball Hall of Fame.

October 24, 1972: Jackie Robinson dies of a heart attack.

Web Sites

Would you like to learn more about Jackie Robinson? Please visit **www.abdopub.com** to find up-to-date Web site links about Jackie Robinson and his baseball career. These links are routinely monitored and updated to provide the most current information available.

Jackie Robinson at his Stamford, Connecticut, home in 1971.

Glossary

balk

An illegal motion made by a pitcher before throwing the ball.

barnstorming

When ball clubs travel from town to town playing games wherever they can find a place to play.

batting average

A measure of how well a baseball player hits the ball. Averages are figured by dividing the number of hits by the number of times at bat.

boycott

To refrain from having any dealings with something in order to make a point or change a condition.

civil rights

The rights guaranteed to every American by the U.S. Constitution.

court-martial

A trial conducted by a military court.

diabetes

A disease in which a person's body cannot properly absorb normal amounts of sugar and starch.

exhibition

A public display. In baseball, exhibition games are played before the actual season begins.

integrate

To make public areas available to people of all races on an equal basis.

National Association for the Advancement of Colored People (NAACP)

An organization founded in 1909 for the purpose of improving the conditions under which African-Americans live.

pennant

An award for the team that wins the championship in its league.

rookie

A player who is in his or her first year of playing on a team.

segregate

To keep races separate from one another.

Index